FORWARD

Nothing can beat the best quality dog food whether you have one dog or rather a lot (like us at Uggeshall Kennels) so these dog treats are not meant in any shape or form to take over the roll of a main meal but simply to enhance, treat and thank your Spaniel for all he does for you (and us).

We have spent years trying to find the best all round food for not only our puppies, the Mothers and Mothers 'to be', our working dogs and our senior ones too. And now we have – so we are proud to say that Uggeshall Dogs and honed, created and powered by Salters Food...

A final note: We would recommend using wheat and gluten free flour for your choice of recipes if your Spaniel is already on either a rice based dog food or a wheat and gluten free one.

Anne-Marie Millard & Richard Botwright

Here at Salters in the wonderful Suffolk countryside, we run a small business and manufacture what we feel to be "The best dog food in the world." With a family history stretching over 3 generations of butchers since 1922, we feel that we are ablely equipped to create these wonderful foods for our dogs. Yes at the end of the day it's a business and has to be treated in the right way, BUT, I do care truly that the ingredients dogs are getting in our foods, are the best, as only the best is good enough. Carefully blended, we put our lovely ingredients together, into a veterinary formulated recipe. When you use the best you get the best results, like your grandmother making a cake! With a quality we believe that is second to none, we have been able to encourage well known breeders, well respected vets, quality stockists and the discerning dog owning public to use Salters, this is proven with the continual compliments from the breeders, vets and the dog owning public, about dogs genuine improvements over and above previous foods, however big the company. It is a great bonus and privilege to us getting recognition, from others as we are really a small company in a huge playing field, but it's a team effort and we all really do appreciate this.
Stephen Salter

SALTERS
PET NUTRITION

info@salterspetfood.com

The Spaniel kitchen diaries

~

JANUARY

Mud is the order of the day outside, throwing one ingenuity test at me after the other. Our Shetland pony Elvis senses weakness as he sees me sliding in a sideward fashion carrying a multitude of laden dog bowls down the hill towards the main kennels.

 He breaks into a canter worthy of The Grand National aiming himself directly in my flight path: his nostrils snorting with pleasure with the idea of spilt dog biscuits for him alone to feast upon. Fortunately the wet condition sees him cantering almost on the spot and he slithers off to annoy the goats instead.

The kitchen hosts a trail of slightly damp scruffy dogs, all burrowing towards the radiator or the warming oven. Ears slightly pricked and nostrils fidgeting as they try and work out if their luck is in for the day – it is. Tango lies across my feet as I work, in this position he knows exactly where I am (I shuffle along the kitchen work surface with him still firmly embedded on my feet); the rest of the sleeping pile can suddenly burst into life if I inadvertently drop a morsel or two. And so we begin.

Cheesy tails

These are rather crumbly so it's not something to shove in your pocket as a training treat, think of them more as a tempting morsel on a bleak day.

INGREDIENTS

- 300 grams wheat and gluten free flour
- 75 grams cheddar cheese (grated)
- 1 tablespoon chopped thyme
- 125 ml olive oil
- 100 ml cold water.

DIRECTIONS

Very simple - mix dry ingredients together first, add the olive oil and then add drips of the water as you mix. For some reason some days you need more water than others.

You need a nice firm-ish dough which you knead on a lightly floured surface. Divide the dough into equal size balls, and then roll them out into equal length 'sticks'.

Place them on a greased baking tray 1 cm apart. Bake in a pre-heated oven 160 degrees C. for about 30 minutes or until golden brown in colour. Remove from oven and leave them to cool.

~

Its thinking about snowing here, the girls are getting over excited about the soft gray sky overhead. The temperature has dropped and suddenly being inside seems the best option for everybody. Sticking my head over the gate and peering down to the kennels there is not a dog in sight, all must be huddled up in their straw beds, snoozing and twitching with the suddenly remembered thoughts of a better days ahead.

We had roast chicken last night and I had dumped the carcass in a saucepan with some water and let it simmer gently away as we ate. On contemplation this morning I realized that I didn't have the energy to make a full chicken soup for us, but did have the will power to make something simple for the dogs. Jade and Myah are with Richard on a shoot and will return home happily complete.

This time of year their life revolves around what Richard is wearing. Seeing the appropriate clothes or catching a glimpse of him methodically cleaning his gun their entire demeanor changes. Bodies become stiff, sitting up as straight as possible, muzzle's shoved skyward almost screaming 'pick me pick ME', Jade almost levitates with contained excitement. As he finally gives them eye contact and a brief nod of the head they are off, flittering with excitement of the day ahead.

When they return home exhausted food is usually the last thing on their mind, however this chicken broth can be ladled (when cool) onto their night time biscuit's to be slurped down before they collapse on their beds: the work they were born to do perfectly executed filling their souls with a total satisfaction.

~

Chicken Broth

INGREDIENTS

- 2 litres of homemade chicken stock (nothing added)
- 2 carrots
- 50g cabbage
- Left over chicken (shredded)
-

DIRECTIONS

Add everything to the pan, and gently bring to a simmer letting the vegetables cook till 'just right'. Take off the heat and leave to cool. What you don't use can be put in a container and left in the fridge or frozen in ice cube trays for another day. Use about 8 tablespoons per meal.

~

Bay is scrithing and scratching again, she has always suffered from very dry skin and during the summer time it seems to alleviate itself, however today she looks miserable so everything I should be doing (cleaning) gets put to one side and we are off to make her some of her own special soap.

BAYS HONEY AND OATMEAL SHAMPOO

Ingredients

1 large mug of natural rolled oats
1 large mug of baking soda
20 drops of essential oil (optional)
1 big tablespoon of runny honey
1 ½ large mug of water

I shove the oats into our ancient magimix to wiz them down a bit. A small child with a mortar and pestle can also work wonders. Tip this lot into a bowl and then add the baking soda gently mixing them together. Drip the oils in now if you are using them: I have far too many from a short lived career choice of a reflexologist. Now add the water slowly mixing it to a batter like paste. Finally add the honey, stirring to thick and creamy.

Now the dog; I can't say Bay likes this experience a lot but today she lets herself go a bit and actually jumps into the bath with a small amount of encouragement. The door is locked behind me to fence off any escape routes down the hall. I pour jugs of warm water over her from her head down. Once soaking wet I lather the concoction all over her and massage it in with my finger nails through to the skin.

After rinsing it off it's out the bath to a clean warm towel which I quickly throw over her with an all in wrestler like skill. I manage to get most of the water off before she eludes my grip and gives herself a darn good shake. With a rather indignant flourish of the head she stalks down the hall leaving a small trail of wet paw prints behind her. As a final fling of independence she jumps onto Billy's favorite chair and has a mammoth roll around on it to finish the drying process off.

As an aside on dry skin Extra Virgin Olive Oil is essential for dry skin. Our 'normal' dog food contains this so best to check yours does too – if not its time to change brands!

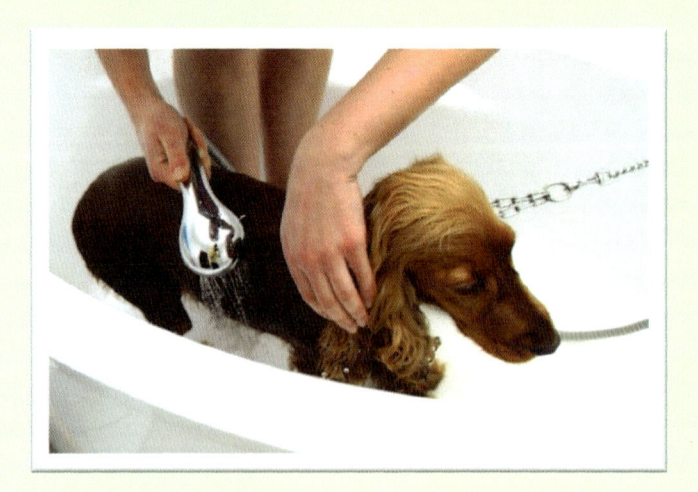

FEBRUARY

This month always gives the glimmer of spring (daffodils poking their noses out) and then slaps you back with ugly weather. In our case, a drizzle of snow covering everything like a fairy tale castle in a snow globe. It is pretty for the short time it is here, but underneath lies acres of surface sludge and a constant need to wash the kitchen floor. I am not sure why we have doors in our home- on giving strict instruction to the smaller people of the household to keep one door shut to the bright snowflaked world outside, they just then manage to leave another door open to the great outdoors. I had just finished mopping myself forward and out of the kitchen door to look behind me to find an interested party of Cockers shuffling along behind me with a very pleased air about them 'look Mum – more footprints for you and, oh, I have also dragged my very wet favorite blanket back indoors too…'

Tangos carrot cake

My handsome boy does love a carrot and my daughters do love leaving one elderly banana behind whilst they start on a fresh bunch, this quick recipe sorts out both.

INGREDIENTS

2 carrots
1 banana
200 grams flour
100 grams rolled oats
50ml sunflower oil
Dribbles of water

DIRECTIONS

Grate the carrots as finely as you can and mash the bananas with a fork. Mix together with the flour, oats and oil and then (if needed) and a splash of water to make a firm dough.

Preheat oven to 180 degrees C. and line a tin with baking parchment.

Flour a surface gently and then roll out the dough to about 1cm thick and then cut these into little squares (roughly 4x4cm) and place on the baking tray.

Bake for 25 minutes and leave to cool overnight (I sometimes leave them in the oven which works best but then I also sometimes forget and turn the over on for something else...).

~

The shooting season has now finished. No more burnished colored pheasants swinging gently in the breeze outside the feed shed, all of Richards's finery have been put away and Jade and Myah are looking a bit woeful. In an attempt to cheer them up and make me feel better about their melancholy I shuffle into the kitchen to make them a favorite treat normally reserved for birthdays.

Mutt loaf

Ingredients:

150g carrots (finely diced)
125g peas (fresh or frozen)
500g minced beef
75g breadcrumbs
2 tablespoons tomato puree
Handful of chopped parsley
3 eggs - hard boiled and peeled.
2 eggs - beaten
125 grams grated cheddar cheese

Cook carrots and peas until soft, drain and leave to cool. Mix the breadcrumbs (if you are using them) with the beef, adding the puree.

Stir in the cooled carrots and peas and then add the beaten eggs. Stir well until all is combined. Roll the mixture into a ball and then divide into two.

Place half the mixture in the base of a greased 1kg loaf tin pressing firmly down into the corners, make a slight channel/dip along the centre line.

Sprinkle dip with grated cheese and then lay the boiled eggs length wise on top of cheese. Place the remaining mixture on top and press firmly down (not crushing eggs though).

Cover with foil and bake in a pre-heated 180c (gas mark 4) oven for 1 - 1 ½ hours. Turn out onto a plate and leave to cool. You can then cut into slices, sprinkle with parsley and serve.

Tango, for all his machismo, is a bit of a light weight if anything hurts. Today's ailment seems to be his paws: his constant quest to root out any available females that I might have hidden from him has seen him burrow under the fence to next doors garden. I know this since after calling for quite a while, then whistling and then shouting I gave up, pulled on wellies and marched out to find him. We came face to face through the fence, him looking woeful and me looking befuddled since I clearly had a problem in how to retrieve him.

Within moments I have a selection of interested on-lookers consisting of a rogue Cockerel, a cat (eyeing said cockerel) and a large selection of dogs from the house since I had either forgotten to shut the door behind me or Eddie the Springer had undone the lock and let them all out.
What happened next was highly ungainly and consisted of a lot of swearing however Tango returned limping to his abode followed by me muttering obscenities and threats to anyone in my wake.

Now to his paws, the single minded obsession had seen him managing to get his pads of the paws stung by early nettles; he is now jumping around like a cat on a hot tin roof and letting out such a squeal of discomfort that most of the house dogs hide under the kitchen table in a worried heap.

I do many things for my dogs and this is one of them. We have a rather attacked Aloe Vera plant in our living room which we use for a multitude of ailments, I tear off a bit, wrestle Tango to the floor and then spend a decent amount of time gently dabbing it into the offending paws. For his credit he does stop shrieking and actually almost fell asleep. The day then returns to a vague sense of normal.

MARCH

It is time to unload the freezer. Since I live in an unjustifiable horror of running out of food in a freak snowstorm that sees us cut off from the world for weeks on end; it leads me to filling the freezer with everything one could imagine the entire family would need in such dark dire days. Now, hopefully, we are past such emergencies so I find myself rooting through the huge chest freezer (bought to hold an entire pig in the days during which I was innocent in such things and it hadn't occurred to me that 'Smokey' and 'Bacon' would actually be cut up and not need a freezer quite so big) and dragging out strange looking bags of goodness knows what. One of these many bags is chopped apples from our tree so I glide indoors feeling efficient for once and start making apple sauce for no particular reason. Having made far too much some of it is going to have to go to the dogs.....

Apple cinnamon muffins

Ingredients

225g Oat Flour
225g brown rice flour
1 tbsp. of baking powder
1 tsp of cinnamon
2 eggs
4 tbsp. runny honey
1 cup applesauce (unsweetened)
¼ cup of sunflower oil

Preheat the oven to 180degrees - combine all the ingredients together and mix thoroughly. Place cupcake papers into a muffin tin. Spoon mixture into papers close to the top. Bake for 18-22 minutes until a sharp knife comes out clean. Remove from oven and let cool completely over a wire rack. Store in an airtight container in the fridge.

I am puppy house training at the moment which basically means I am adding more chaos to an already chaotic household. Things materialize and disappear in this chasm of a home with such odd regularity that it is all quite normal. One of my daughters (actually virtually always Matilda) will appear in front of me in an outfit I have never seen before; 'where did you get that from?' I enquire, 'it was in my wardrobe' is the answer and that is the end of that.

Socks are so constantly eaten or reassembled or hidden by dogs that I virtually have a monthly set up re-order on Amazon for school socks. I have just, quite simply, given up trying to win that particular battle.

The puppies means that there is even more chance of wee around the house than normal; the majority of the time a bottle of bitter apple spray (Amazon again) works a treat but since we do have a labyrinth of a home puppies are now weeing on the carpet (much to my displeasure) however much I try and keep doors shut and stairgates closed. We actually have more stair gates now than we did when the children were tiny. These days they can just vault over them, talking on a mobile phone and eating an apple at the same time. Clearly going to be good multi taskers when they are adults.

There will always be one puppy that manages to get their head stuck in the railings of the stair gate. The shriek of sheer blinding panic that can come from one trapped puppy is unbelievable. It will be so shrill it will be heard in the next county and it makes every member of the family start running in a blind panic to find the source of the noise.
For some reassurance I can tell you most of the time what happens is the puppy inserts their head into the rails sideways, turns back to normal and then tries to pull back quickly finding out that they are apparently stuck. All that needs to be done is to get the pup (top tip this) to realign its head to the same angle as it was when it was inserted and hey presto you are released!
Anyway back to the puddles of pee on the carpet – good old baking soda rubbed into said puddle quickly dissipates it and it long lasting odour....now for something else that smells..

Herby fish hearts

Ingredients

100 grams fish (tinned tuna is our favorite)
3 tablespoons freshly chopped herbs
2 tablespoons extra virgin olive oil
1 egg
200 grams flour
100 grams ground hazelnuts (you can omit this and just add extra flour)

Preheat oven to 180 degrees. Line a baking tray with baking parchment. Puree the fish and herbs in a food processor. Put the puree in a bowl and then stir in olive oil and egg. Add the flour and nuts and mix to smooth dough. Shape into a ball, wrap in Clingfilm and let it rest for 30 minutes.

On a floured surface, roll out the dough until about 8mm thick. With a biscuit cutter, cut out little heart shapes (or whatever you have to hand). Place on the baking tray and let bake for 30 minutes.
Let them cool on a wire rack and store in a biscuit tin. Voila!!

~

Final idea for the month — empty plastic bottles make great play things for pups. Make sure you take off the wrapper, lid and plastic bit around the lid first and chuck the bottle on the floor. Hours of VERY noisy but cheap fun. Good excuse to have another gin and tonic in my book.

APRIL

Oh I love this month – it's the start of all the blossom on the orchard trees. The plum blossom has already been and gone with a huge sigh, leaving drifts of delicate white snow on the ground. But now the sugar candy cherry blossom are peeping through followed closely by the apples, cherries and the pears. Daffodils that have stood the test of time now jostle alongside the bluebells and wild primrose edging the gardens and orchard.

Elvis now has a spring in his step and is cantering perfect figure of eights, doing flying changes like a seasoned dressage horse not the fat little Shetland he is. To finish the show he lies down at the top of the hill and rolls in a higgledy piggledy fashion down towards the hay munching goats that look suitably impressed and wander over to congratulate him on his prowess.

The dogs are happy now since the house doors remain open and they can come and go as they please not worrying about getting their paws muddy (which I am sure concerns them a great amount), this means I am not followed about my spaniel bodyguards quite as much as in the wetter and colder months.

Feeling a spring in my step I decide to be extra generous and make something that with some oozing ingredients, all the more forbidden since not only am I now wheat and gluten intolerant I now can't eat dairy either..

PIZZA SQUARES

These squares always remind of mini pizzas, those delicious tempting morsels wafting melting cheese scent all over the house....

100 grams flour
100 grams course oats
2 eggs
75 grams finely grated cheese
75 grams finally diced ham
100 ml water

Preheat the oven to 180 degree C. Line a baking sheet with baking parchment.

Mix all the ingredients together to make smooth dough. Cover this and let it rest for about 30 minutes.

On a floured surface, roll out the dough to about (maximum) 1 cm thickness and cut into rectangles 3cm by 5cm. Place these on the baking sheet and bake for about 25 minutes. Turn off the heat and let the biscuits harden for another two hours. Store in an airtight container.

~

I have now just proved to the world in general that my brain cannot hold all the pieces of information shoved into it - and it has all to do with the cats. Fortunately Tilly is at least attempting to save my sanity by accosting the vet friend and her daughter in the school playground mornings with varying questions on feline reproduction. She (Tilly) is now a mine of information and I am just hoping she is not running up a serious vet bill for me in the meantime.

MUMMY! These dulcet tones of my nine year old ring out of the clamoring children at the end of the school day, 'That odd noise that Delilah is making means that she is in season!!!'. We hurry home in a vain attempt to catch Delilah in the house before she goes off on one of her lengthy forays through the rape fields. Too late.

In the meantime I return to the kitchen and am quickly sidetracked by the fact that 'someone' has left the fridge door open and I have a queue of the younger dogs waiting their turn to raid it. Tango is sitting on his chair looking woefully pious. Finding a half-eaten pot of yoghurt with definite signs of munching around the rim I set upon putting together a quick snack for my beloved boy.

For the record my other beloved boy Billy was found with a piece of cold roast beef slowly being chomped down – not so well behaved!

Feeling fruity

Ingredients

1 apple finely sliced
50 grams dried apricots finally chopped
25 grams dates finally chopped
100 ml of low fat yoghurt
1 teaspoon honey

Place all the fruits into a bowl and mix in the yoghurt and the honey. Serve over regular food or just use it as a tasty healthy snack (for your dog, not you!!

We do get close up and personal with our dogs. Apart from spending the days wandering round chatting to them all in passing some of them are allowed to sleep on the beds (or we are allowed to sleep on their beds is a bit more likely) so we can often wake up with a Spaniel nose to nose with us.

Tango is a particular offender of this, although he does prefer sitting on my head in the night like a rather interesting foxy coloured hat. When pushed off he slides down to lick my nose. On consideration that he keeps his working tools especially clean with a thorough slurping lick-fest it not something I relish really. On noticing stinky breath the following treats really do work.

After dinner mints

These as designed as doggie breath fresheners - they might look a bit odd but the dogs don't seem to notice! I buy the activated charcoal from the health food shop (or chemist) in capsule form and then break it open. If I do it by myself it's nice and neat, if Tilly helps me it's not quite as neat....

Ingredients:

200 grams flour
25 grams of chopped mint
10 grams of parsley
1 tablespoon of activated charcoal
3 tablespoons of olive oil
250 ml approximately of cold water

Preheat the oven to 180 degrees (350f) or gas mark 4.

Combine the flour, herbs and activated charcoal in a bowl. Mix in the olive oil and start to add the cold water gradually until you have smooth dough. Rub into 1cm balls and place on a greased baking tray.

Put them in the pre heated oven for 25-30 minutes. Remove from baking sheet and place on a wire rack to cool down. These can store in an air tight tub for up to four weeks.

MAY

Perfection (nearly anyway)....we have sun and warm grass under our toes. The tulips are standing saluting the sky, their petals arching upwards as to catch the sun stream as nectar. All is quiet for a few hours on end as the dogs in the kennels snooze in the warmth of the day, Myah is curled up in her bed with her nose resting in the doorway, her straw is cool and the water bucket close by. The Cockers lay in an upside down heap, spread eagled to the light, their lower lips flopping open as they fall into a deeper sleep. Sally and Elly are keeping a close eye on me; I am the bringer of fun, the walk to the river in the adjacent field.

The children and I venture quietly forth (quite hard to be quiet with these two), slide open the bolt to Sally and Elly's kennel to find two bright eyed undulating Springers knowing what's coming next.
Off to the river. There is nothing like splashing around in a river on a warm sultry day. Even though it is only May the grass in the field is long and dry, we can flop into it giggling as the Springers disappear off at speed to the water's edge. PLOP. In they go and we follow. We spend a good hour there, climbing the banks, trying to make a bridge, falling in and generally escaping from daily reality for a short while and then trek back to the house to investigate what mayhem had been attempted whilst we were gone.

Theo has completely rearranged the kitchen in a relative short time. Some dogs stack the food bowls up for me - not Theo though. He has decided (probably with some help) to overturn the water bowl and spend a while making ever increasing circles of wet paw prints obviously followed by an attempt to mop up his handy work with the soft pillows from my beloved chair.....apron on and onwards with some cooking after a decent while spent clearing up the mess muttering under my breath.

Ginger dogs

We are very keen on Apple cider vinegar in this house for ourselves but it is also very good for your canine friends too. You can make these treats or even put some in your dog's water. Start with just a drip and increase the amount gradually (it is an acquired taste!) until you get up to about a teaspoon a day (take a glug yourself if you have not tried it….) to the water.

Apple cider vinegar is good for arthritis, allergies, itchy skin, eliminating tear stains, fighting fleas and other pests and lots more.

Ingredients:

550 grams flour
1 tsp of baking powder
1 tsp ground ginger
1 tsp cinnamon
½ tsp baking soda
1 egg
60 ml sunflower oil
2 big tablespoons of molasses
1 big tablespoon of peanut butter
1 tablespoon of apple cider vinegar

Preheat oven to 180 degrees. Combine all the ingredients together and mix thoroughly until a dough forms. Sometimes I add more peanut butter if the dough seems too solid and more flour if it seems a bit 'wet'.

Your dough needs to be of a consistency that you roll out onto a lightly floured surface without it sticking. Roll it so it is roughly ¼ inch thick and use whatever cutter shape you have to hand.

Place on an ungreased baking sheet and bake for 18-22 minutes until the edges are golden brown. Let them completely cook down on a wire rack and then store in air tight container at room temperature.

This time of year our country lanes are plagued by kamikaze rabbits of the miniature kind. They shoot out across the road in front of you as you drive with trepidation, this is always followed by 'oh look.....soooooo sweet' chiming from the back seats as I do my best not to kill them (again). This treat is in honour of the fallen few.

Bunny snacks

300 grams flour
1 egg - beaten
1 banana - mashed
2 tbs honey
3 tbs olive oil
2 tbs cold water

Mix all the ingredients in a large mixing bowl until they form a dough. Add a little water drip by drip if you feel the dough is to firm to roll. Knead the dough on a lightly floured surface and then roll to 5mm thick. We obviously use a rabbit shape cookie cutter to make ours but that's up to you!

Transfer the cookies onto a lightly oiled baking tray about 1cm apart and brush with a little more beaten egg.

Bake in a preheated oven at 160 degrees C. or gas mark 3 for 15-20 minutes.

Put on wire tray to cool. You can decorate these if you are feeling artistic…..we use low fat cream cheese mixed with some olive oil and then put in a piping bag. This can make quite fun fluffy white tails, ears and eye for your confections.

I love Billy, he is my hero in many ways, he lies at the foot of the bed guarding me with hooded eyes, partially asleep but partly awake for one of those 'just in case' moments. If anything untoward happens he is immediately up and barking, waking up the entire household usually for the simple reason likes a cat knocking something over in the kitchen below.

But he does get itchy ears which he tries to avoid showing me since he hates them being cleaned – however recently I have tried a new method – warm olive oil, which he does rather like (won't admit it but doesn't run off and hide). I gently heat the oil so it's 'barely' warm, put a lead on Bill and pull him gently in between my legs as I sit at the kitchen table. From here I use a teaspoon of oil for each ear, pouring it in as softly as I can, folding the ear flap over and massaging it in so I can hear a general squishing noise from beneath. I swop over ears as quickly as I can to avoid the dreaded head shake and repeat on the other side.

He is still looking at me with woeful face as I let go and he stomps off shaking his head like an embarrassed teenage boy having received a kiss from his mum in public. Same thing tomorrow I tell him as he disappears to oust someone from his favorite chair.

Liver fudge

Ingredients

400 grams liver (chicken/pig/lamb)
300 ml cold water
400 grams flour
150 grams cooked green beans
1 egg
65 ml extra virgin olive oil

Puree the liver and the water in a food processor. Chop the beans into 5mm pieces and put the whole lot in a mixing bowl. Add the flour and olive oil till you have a smooth paste.

Put all the mixture into an 18x28cm shallow baking tin lined with baking parchment and then cook in a preheated oven (180 degrees'. Or gas mark 4) for 30-35 minutes.
Prick with a fork halfway through cooking to release the air. It is cooked when an inserted knife comes out clean. Leave to cool on a wire rack.

Once cool you can cut into 2.5cm squares with a sharp knife. Place all your squares into resalable freezer bags and freeze until needed. These are great training treats and freeze/defrost very well.

JUNE

The month starts like it means to go on. Puppy leaving days for me are a tad tense, it's like first day back at school; in that case I feel as long as my daughters manage to return (actually I am talking about tilly here since Tabitha is at an age where she can get herself looking more presentable than I have ever managed even as an adult) to school clean, ironed, hair brushed and not covered in dog hairs I am on a winner. It's downhill from then onward.

And I am going off at yet another tangent. So puppy leaving days mean clean puppies, ear inspections, all paperwork appropriate and in the right order and then all is left is making sure I am handing over the right puppy to the right person. First lot of handovers done, I begin to greet the second family only to be distracted by Tilly running past carrying a bowl of water (warm) and squealing 'towels towels towels'......she reappears a moment later from MorMor's part of the house clad in the shortest shorts ever, a pajama top and no shoes. 'It's all ok Mummy, it's going to be fine, don't worry we are handling it...'

It transpired that Delilah was giving birth......we had been too late....

The rest of the day was punctuated by my daughters running in and out giving us all updates on the birthing process....'one more Mummy, one more Mummy..can we keep it?' and so on. To give them credit they both did the whole process themselves, watching me with the pups over the years has apparently paid off.

By the time the last pup had left we had four fluffy kittens, one looking slightly more bedraggled than the others. On enquiring why this one looked the way it did it was explained that they had been enlightened to the birthing in the first place by MorMor squealing 'Tilly Tilly – I have just sat on something wet' (you do need to understand and forgive my mother for this since she is partially sighted these days). The something wet happened to be the first kitten Delilah popped out onto MorMor sofa whom is now named 'Hamster'......

~

This time of year sees me grooming and flea combing the dogs outside on the grass. The ones that love it (Bubbles) lye happily waiting their turn, already upside down and legs akimbo. The ones that don't like it (Billy) go and hide in a very dark place. It is the time of year for fleas so the following treats can work well but give your dog not the best breath in the world.

Flea Fighters

Ingredients

250 grams flour
1 teaspoon of brewer's yeast
½ teaspoon chopped garlic
3 tbs olive oil
75 ml cold water

Combine the flour, brewer's yeast and garlic in a large mixing bowl. Mix in the olive oil and add the measured water a dribble at a time until you have a smooth dough.

Roll the mixture out into a sausage shape and cut into two cm lengths. With the palm of your hand roll them into little balls and then squish them down a little with a back of a fork. Place on a greased baking sheet and into a pre heated oven (180 degrees C or gas mark 4) and bake for 20-25 minutes. Leave to cool on a rack and then place in an airtight container.

It's now cherry picking time unless the birds get to them first. Getting and eating these little beauties are a prefect family pastime. I shove the kids up the tree and they pass them down to me. Voila!

In the meantime when I am 'sans' children (they do have rope ladders to aid descent by the way) I have to fend for myself. Eating cherries straight from a tree has to be one of the perfect moments ever. I have tried the cherry picker which works to a point – I just end up getting mainly bits of tree and bark in my eyes and hair – but I find launching my body upwards and grabbing a branch whilst keeping my chin to my chest to avoid getting anything in my eyes many look extremely silly but works.

My only audience is usually Teddy and Ernie who both are very good at looking slightly bewildered. Since I am now complete with cherries I am off to have a healthy lunch to make me feel even more pious. My larder is full of stuff I buy on a rare trip to a health food store – being wheat, gluten and dairy free myself does make me feel a little envious when I watch the family tuck into my homemade bread, Yorkshire puddings followed by extra creamy ice cream.

My expensive exotic shop often spends most of its life on the shelf in the larder but at least I feel oddly better about it when I see the coconut oil next to the brown rice flour...the next recipe is a perfect feel and look good one (even for you!) which for me has some store cupboard basics as ingredients (check expiration date though if you fall into my category).

120 grams oat flour
120 grams brown rice flour
100 grams flaxseeds
3 tablespoons sesame seeds
1 egg
½ cup water

Preheat the oven to 180 degrees C. Combine all the ingredients and mix thoroughly until a dough forms. Roll the dough out on a lightly floured surface to 1cm thick. Now use a cookie cutter of your choice to cut out shapes. Put on a baking sheet not too close together since they can spread and place in oven for 20-25 minutes until golden brown. Remove from oven and leave to cool completely on a wire rack. Store in an airtight container in the fridge.

JULY

My beautiful cutting garden is now beginning to overflow with flowers. It is my perfect present from Richard who starts planning it in the dark days through to its fruition and beyond. We start with sweet peas, the old fashioned heavily scented ones climbing up the walls of the old greenhouse filling the air with the heaviest of aromas. Next the delicate Cosmos followed by the mass of Dahlias, these are from deep bowls of amethyst to small pompoms of vibrating orange curling in amongst the lime green Zinnias to set all the shades off in their own personal vibrancy. I couldn't ask for more.....fortunately the cutting garden is fenced in so I don't have any help picking the flowers from my four legged friends. It is also the hideaway of our raspberry bushes which makes flower picking time take a tad longer.

The old garden walls are now heavy with honeysuckle and creeping roses, a walk round the orchard is awash with differing scents wafting in a summer breeze. I sit on my rickety bench under the plum tree with my eyes half shut and breathe in the magic. Teddy and Ernie are close by and are watching me. Both are well versed in my body language so neither are moving in the heat of the day. They are flopped out like old fashioned fire-side rugs but suddenly awake as I re approach carrying their favorite summer treat.

Double crunch cubes

3 cups f plain nonfat yoghurt
1 cup of peanut butter (unsalted)
1 tablespoon of honey

Combine all the ingredients and mix thoroughly. Tip into ice cube trays and freeze solid. Pop out a cube or two as needed.

~

Our cats are now taking over the house. Or, to be more exact, taking over my Mothers part of the house. As you could have guessed we kept the kittens and since they were born on MorMor's sofa that to them means that they own the place (and her).

It is my favorite part of the house. Once those walls were filled with clanging and clattering and puffs of smoke from the blacksmiths bellows. Those walls must be able to tell some wonderful tales. These days the rooms are cluttered (in a very artistic fashion) with my Mothers and my late Father's life. Paintings cover the walls, the old bellows and fire place house a collection of driftwood, ceramics, drawings from Tabitha and Matilda, vases overflowing with flowers in the warmer months. From there you are followed by the curious eyes of many a Steiff teddy bear and Victorian dolls remnants of one of my Mothers past careers.

The bears sit in old hatboxes clutching collections of old lace and dolls clothes. Books are stuffed in every orifice, my paintings from primary school and family photos jostle alongside an elderly gramophone. The cats now sleep in a 1920's doll prams or up in the loft space alongside my Fathers collection of trains and boats that he spent decades crafting by hand. Occasionally a train will come crashing down onto the sofa from the height above – I like to think of it as my dad making some point about something we are not doing correctly in his eyes.

Tails droop off the loft stair case, a sensible place to be since Bubbles feels every cat needs a thorough daily clean or she won't have done her duty. I can sit on the sofa (out the way of impending concussion – I have learnt my lesson) and take it our entire family history. It really is a magnificent place to be.

The cats, on catching sight of me, rush and hide just in case I am on a de-worming mission. Shiny beacons of eyes resonate from under a sofa or in amongst Bubbles huge fluffy ears (she does have her uses) until they are reassured I am just passing through or carrying something of delight for their palates. The smell of the next treats has their fur standing on end and I fill little old plates for them with all the crumbs.

Tuna thins

1 can tuna fish in natural juice (water)
4 tbs olive oil
1 egg
2 teaspoons dried herbs
250 grams cornflour
150 grams rolled oats
50 grams of flour

Drain the tuna in a sieve. Then puree it with the oil and the egg in a blender.

Mix the puree with the other ingredients to make a dough. Roll out the dough to about 1cm thick and cut into whatever shapes take your fancy.

Place on a baking sheet and bake for about 25 minutes in a preheated 180 degree oven. Store in a biscuit tin.

We finish the month with runny tummies from the younger dogs. At present it is probably something they have investigated if it had any devouring possibilities (frogs they had discovered are not at all tasty) but their tails are wagging, eyes are shining but I am trying to clear up pools of sludge. So it's on to the tried and tested technique of yoghurt from our fridge (plain low fat stuff so always left by the kids and not eaten in a midnight raid). It is a great probiotic with sources of calcium and zinc. The bigger dogs will eat it from their normal meals (a tablespoon per day) but the little ones look at their bowels covered in an unknown substance, look at me and that's about it. So I resort to letting them lick it off the spoon……

First its 24 hours off food – I am met by annoyed and affronted faces as they queue up for supper. I am told off by the fact they decided wee-ing into my wellies I left outside was significant punishment for me. The next day we are on to 'bland' food for them. Cooled boiled rice (2 parts) and chopped cooled chicken (1 part). This is wolfed down though the rice part does tend to be spread across the kitchen floor. Learning to eat rice is a rite of passage for them all. Over the days I change the ratio to more chicken less rice and then start adding bits of their daily kibble to it. After a day or so or 'poo' watch they seem back to normal. More than a couple of days of this though would be a vet visit.

AUGUST

We are now upon the 'dog days of summer' did you know that? From late July to mid-August sees Sirius the Dog Star rising alongside the sun. The term *cuniculares dies* was coined by the Romans who saw these phenomena and thought the brightness of the star contributed to the heat of the sun. There you go – a new fact to share with your canine companions as you make the next treat.

Lick a lolly...

You can eat these too...

INGREDIENTS

100ml apple juice
100 ml cranberry juice

Or

Home made chicken stock

Combine and freeze in lolly moulds adding a rawhide chew stick as opposed to a standard lolly stick.

Theo is quite determined that little Nevil cannot own his own bed, hence whatever I give Nevil to sleep on in the kitchen at night gets dragged off and hidden by Theo during the day. I have tried solid beds; these are just turned upside down with Nevil still in them, his little worried eyes peeping out like a giant tortoise making sure the coast was clear

.A big soft and heavy sheepskin bed was next. This caused even greater delight since Theo took to pulling it up to the top of the wooden stairs and then using it as a toboggan to wend his way down at speed. Hysterical to watch but I could feel the vets bills adding up in my head as I did so this idea instantly had the plug pulled on it.

Finally Nevil now has his own private cage in the laundry room from which he can eye the cat that lives above the downstairs loo and bark at it too. It is far too heavy for Theo to dog-handle and too small for him to invade. So far so good.

~

Flower power

INGREDIENTS
240 grams whole-wheat flour
180 grams of plain sunflower seeds
65 grams of oat bran
4 tablespoons runny honey
3 tablespoons applesauce (no sugar)
1 egg
Water.

Combine all the dry ingredients first, and then add the honey and apple sauce finishing off by using the water in drips to make a firm dough.
Roll out on a lightly floured surface until 1cm thick and use a cookie cutter of your choice.
Place on a baking tray and put in a preheated oven at 180 degrees or gas mark 4.
Bake for 20-25 minutes and then let cool on a wire tray.

It is truly summer, how magnificent! The dogs are snoozing in the sun barely bothering to bark at any marauding pheasants wandering past them. The lighter ones are having sunscreen applied to their delicate noses, once they have worked out it doesn't taste very nice they stop trying to lick it off each other or themselves. As we leave for a trip to the beach (minus dogs) we note that most of them have meandered under the cool respite of the trees shadows, and there they must have laid since on returning home with two wet and sand blasted children they don't seem to have moved a muscle. Time now for afternoon tea under our ancient apple tree in the Orchard thus inspiring the next recipe.

An apple a day...

Our apple trees are now abundant with fruit so it makes sense not to waste any....(hard job)...you can make these apple rings for yourselves or use them as a treat.

INSTRUCTIONS

1. Wash, peel and core apples.
2. Slice the apples thinly and evenly.

3. Pat the slices dry if need be.
4. the slices on wire baking or cooling racks and position in the oven.
5. Set oven to the lowest temperature and prop the door open with a wooden spoon if you can to allow the moisture to escape from the oven.
6. Bake for 5 to 8 hours. Times vary due to humidity levels, ovens, apple varieties, slice thickness etc. so just keep checking.
7. Check apples for any moisture inside and out. The slices should feel dry and leathery on the outside without any tackiness. Tear a slice in half to see if there is any moisture on the inside – it should feel like a dry dense sponge.
8. Allow to cool completely before storing in an airtight container.

SEPTEMBER

We are now groaning under the weight of fresh produce from the kitchen garden. Large bundles of vegetables now appear through the kitchen window at a regular pace and left on the counter for me to deal with. In the meantime I am also struggling to find things. I have no idea why Cockers like 'transporting' personal items around the house (and outdoors too if possible) but the combination of myself getting older and more forgetful mixed in with a thoughtful Cocker or two (Theo, Tango, Nevil and Jade to be precise) collecting whatever they feel I might be in need of (car keys for one) finds me often stomping around the house getting increasingly stressed desperately trying re locate something that either I have 'lost' or one of the dogs have dispatched themselves on an important mission to find me, got distracted leaving said object in an obscure place and then forgetting their original mission themselves. Not at all helpful!

So it goes like this: I walk into the kitchen, stop, now having to think exactly why I am in the kitchen. Mind appears blank so I turn and retrace my steps hoping to have my memory jolted, in my wake follows my motley crew: Nevil eyes shining with the prospect of something possibly interesting happening, Theo now carrying someone's bed, Tango with Tilly's school reading book and Jade with one sock sticking out of her mouth as she munches on it....

Having made everything possible with our courgette glut I now turn to making something for the dogs. With the heavy scent of vinager left over from our chutney making I gently shuffle all the dogs out of the kitchen to have some peace and quiet whilst I turn my hand to some new delicacy for the dogs to delight in.

Courgette bread

INGREDIENTS

140 grams flour
2 tsp baking powder
1 tsp cinnamon
3 eggs
3 tablespoons honey
2 cups pureed courgettes
60 ml sunflower oil

Peel, slice and puree the courgettes in a food processor.
Combine all the ingredients together and mix thoroughly. Lightly grease a bread tin and spoon mixture into it - doesn't matter if it's close to the top the bread will not rise much.

Bake in a preheated oven for 20-25 minutes or until a knife gently inserted comes out clean.
Remove from oven and let it cool completely on a wire rack.
Store in an airtight container in the fridge.

The apple trees are in full force now. No sitting under them unless you care to be bonked on the head by a falling fruit. The dogs are in heaven; to them this is not an apple tree but a tennis ball tree laden with joy specifically meant for them. If we care to while away a few moments of rest in a deck chair we will wake to find a sea of apples planted at our feet surrounded by a set of very pleased Spaniels eagerly looking at their stash first and then a quick pointed look at us with furious wagging tails to amplify the point. If we do not respond then another frantic hunt will be undertaken to find us the perfect prize to dump in our laps....whilst they go and re stock a fresh batch I disappear off with some of the fruit tucked into my t shirt bottom to go and make some good use of it.

Apple dumplings

INGREDIENTS
1 apple
1 carrot
150 grams spelt flour
150 grams course rolled oats
2 eggs
3 tablespoons molasses
Water and flour as needed

Finely grate the apple and carrot then mix with the other ingredients slowly added the water and extra flour as needed to make an easily shaped not too sticky dough.

Preheat the oven to 180 degrees C. and line a baking tray with parchment.

Use two tea spoons to make little dumpling shapes and place on the baking sheet as you go. Bake for 30 minutes and then turn off the oven letting the dumplings cool and dry whilst still in the oven.

Store in a paper bag.

Suffolk in September (and often October) really is at its most beautiful. The sunlight hangs low washing the countryside with a deep golden glow, the bushes and trees are hung with fruit, flowers and berries. The air is heavy with scent of every kind and my flower garden over flows with luxury. We are almost drugged with over whelming assault on the senses: sight of drooping roses with tear drops of morning dew, wafts of scent and the sensuous bath of sunlight and gentle breeze. Perfection.

~

Pasta Perfect

INGREDIENTS

200 grams cooked gluten free pasta
200 grams low fat cottage cheese
200 grams low fat natural yoghurt
6 chopped basil leaves
50 grams French beans -chopped finely
200 grams cooked boneless chicken
2 tbs olive oil

Mix all the ingredients in a large bowl and then pour into a 28" x 20" oven proof dish.

Bake in a preheated oven at 200 degrees C. for 15 - 20 minutes. Leave to cool thoroughly.

Cut the bake e up into 3" inch squares and freeze 3 or 4 squares per bag. These can then be individually defrosted as and when you need them (just add only 3-4 squares per meal).

OCTOBER

It's not that one of my daughters is accident prone but steps and inanimate objects are especially good at impeding her speedy path leading to various squeals, cuts, sores, hysterical shrieking etc...we always have hibiscrub on hand for the animals but if I can't pass it off as a human product said child refuses to be treated it with. This is probably down to the fact that when she was very small and been treated with an animal intended solution one of her siblings followed her round all day neighing and woofing......I shall say no more on this subject. However there is a homemade cleaning solution that works for small children, adults and animals alike.

1 pint of cooled boiled water
½ teaspoon of cooking salt
½ teaspoon of calendula tincture (if you have it)

Mix and clean wound every five hours for the first 24 hours......

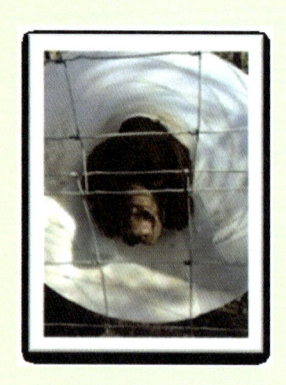

Beautiful broccoli

INGREDIENTS

120 grams oat flour
120 grams brown rice flour
120 grams cooked chicken shredded
120 grams pureed broccoli
(about a cup)
2 tbs molasses
1 egg
Water as needed

First puree the broccoli in the food processer and then add the chicken. Combine the rest of the ingredients adding the water dribble by dribble to make a firm dough.
From here you can either roll out the dough to 1-2 cm thick and use a cookie cutter or make the dough into small balls. Place these on a lined baking sheet and bake in a preheated oven at 180 degrees C. for approx. 25 minutes or until golden brown. Remove from tray and let cool completely on a wire rack.

I find it impossible to cook 'just enough', whatever I attempt to make in a frugal manner still ends up looking like I am preparing a banquet for Henry V111. Depending on the time of year the table groans under the weight of vegetables and fruits from Richards hard work; not that the dogs complain. Billy, now being main man of the house, has first choice of leftover food items. If you don't offer if it to him he will just do his best to nab it from your plate on its way to the sink (I know, I know, he should not behave like that but he does and it, as always, is my fault). His firm favorites though are Indian food and cleaning up the roasting pans before they go to be washed.

Tabby and Matilda do all the washing up themselves now and, after muttering to each other that none of their friends do this; usually carry on in a happy haphazard fashion....'it's not clean!! Wash it again Tilly!!' ...yes it is clean! Look if I give to Billy he doesn't lick it therefore it is clean' comes the retort. If I stick my head through the window (Richard and I are now outside cleaning the runs) I get a barrage of complaints from both of them about each other so I try to sneak past so they don't see me.

The 'indoor' dogs get the leftovers on their dinners whilst the 'outdoor' ones get my following recipe. Both lots seem happy with the arrangement.

Lovely leftovers

INGREDIENTS

2/3 flour of choice
1/3 rolled oats

Pureed carrots
Pureed broccoli
Pureed squash

1 egg
Water

This recipe comes from our leftovers - so I change the ratio of ingredients depending on what we have left over. I take the cooked cold vegetables (no butter or seasoning on them) and puree them in the food processor.

I them pour this into a big mixing bowl and add the egg first to begin binding and then add the oats and flour to make a dough that's still a little sticky but still holds its own form.

From here I drop little balls of the mixture using two desert spoons onto a lightly greased baking tray and then bake in an oven preheated t 180 degree C for about 20 minutes until golden brown.

Place on a wire rack to cool.

OCTOBER

Despite the darkening nights and the pitch black mornings our home does lend itself well to the winter months. The dogs huddle around the kitchen stove or flat out and snoring to the ever burning fire places (of which we have many). My Mother is a part time pyro maniac according to Richard; she begins her potbellied stove preparation almost straight after her now normal 'late' breakfast. This requires gathering lots of little sticks and pine cones and sending her granddaughters out to bring in buckets full of coal. From this she creates a crackling pit of fire, sometimes with the unintentional effect of flames shooting out the chimney, startling passersby to pull their cars over and come charging to the door in a panic. We (Richard and I) have tempered this enthusiasm now though – even though it was funny (to us) at the time and we did thank the startled couple at the door profusely but I have a nagging worry about fire in general so I leave our fire building to the man of the house....

The kitchen now dances in only the candle light; one for the sheer romance of it all and secondly so I don't become too aware of the carpet of muddy paw prints decorating my beloved space of a kitchen. It's a good time of year to cook, during summer months I feel I should be outside doing 'stuff' but this time of year the house needs to be filled with hearty smells and warming scents.

Squashams

INGREDIENTS

200 grams oat flour
200 grams brown rice flour
½ teaspoon cinnamon
½ teaspoon nutmeg
½ teaspoon ginger
1 egg
3 tablespoons unsweetened apple sauce
Cooked pumpkin flesh - pureed
A few tablespoons of water

Combine all the ingredients together apart from the water. Add the water slowly to make a consistency that can be table spooned and dropped onto a baking tray (un greased).

The cookies will not rise or flatter so you can press them down with the back of your spoon if you so desire.

Put in a preheated oven at 180 degrees centigrade and bake for 18 - 22 minutes until golden brown. Let them cool completely on a wire rack before putting them in an air tight container.

~

The only problem with this time of year is the fireworks blasting off all over the place. Fortunately none are very close by but still to the dogs it can be a very unnerving experience. Poor Tango is the worst affected, whereas some of them just go and hide in or under anything they can find, Tango is absolulty, 100 per cent fixated on sitting on my head. Fine, obviously when you are lying down, but not fine if you are sitting in a chair. He uses my legs as a step ladder, my stomach as a spring board whilst shoveling his nose into my neck.

It is a very cumbersome painful procedure for me but however hard I try to just simply cuddle him, he won't take no for an answer, so I find myself lying on the living room floor or sofas whilst he fidgets around snuffling into my hair and rearranging himself on my face. Thank goodness I love him to pieces.

93

Crescent moons

INGREDIENTS

3 large boiled potatoes
150 grams cooked pumpkin puree
100 grams sausage meat

100 grams whole-wheat flour
3 tbs vegetable oil
1 egg
50 grams sesame seeds

Put the potatoes through a potato ricer, mix in the pumpkin and sausage meat.
Now add the flour, oil and the egg and knead all the ingredients to make smooth dough. Cover and let rest for 30 minutes.. Preheat the oven to 180 degrees C.
On a floured surface roll out the dough to about 1cm thick and use a cookie cutter to make 'moon' shapes (or whatever takes your fancy!). Place on a baking sheet and decorate with the seeds.
Bake for 25 minutes and allow to cool and dry in the oven for 2 hours.

Finding the weather still quite mild but with a certain 'whoosh' in the wind the outside dogs are findng themselves various things to do (which they shouldn't) whilst Richard is out shooting. This leaves me in charge and since I am rather a soft touch I seem to spend a lot of time covering their tracks. There are always one or two who are in a bit of a sulk that today was not their 'chosen' day to accompany Richard thus making them even more mischievous.

The main game is digging....or burrowing more to be precise. Sally can often be found with just her butt stuck up in the air and the rest of her down a dusty hole. She is not the only one but certainly the best – the scenario goes like this...Sally spends several hours burrowing under her kennel and then I spend quite a while filling it back in Her best achievement was when she created an actual escape route from her kennel to next door and I was greeted by the wrong dogs in the wrong kennels. It took me more than a moment to work that one out.

The other dogs clearly hold her skill in great magnitude and are often found in an appreciative gaggle admiring her at work. Some do copy but not quite to her level of skill as of yet.

Since Richard normally returns home in a very genial mood I can easily quickly mention 'in passing' what or who I have managed to not get quite right in the general scheme of things before I distract him elsewhere.

Anyway it does seem like a harmless pastime, dusty and dirty but it seems to keep them all amused whether they are involved or just in the audience in general.

DECEMBER

This is obviously my children's favorite time of year but the dogs seem to get caught up in the flurry of festive preparations too....I don't think they know exactly why they are excited (dogs that is) but they are.

Being Nevils first Christmas he is particularly enjoying helping with the decorating. He struts on past carrying various things in his mouth, tail bolt upright with pride, I take whatever he is carrying away from him, put it on my ever expanding pile of confiscated decorations and off he trots to find the next piece of festive fancy he can lay his little paws on.

Even the puppies in the kennels are getting over excited. One in particular has learnt the skill of a fast escape. There is always one, but this one is better than most. I open the gate to the run carrying the bowls of breakfast; he clambers up and over shrieking 'I'm free! I'm free! I don't know where I am going but I am free none the less!' and off he goes in a sideways gallop towards the house, quick duck past Tango, underneath Billy's belly and into the kitchen. As long as he doesn't met the sentinel guard of the kitchen (Jade) he is ok. If he does he is frog marched back to where he belongs and repositioned with his colleagues in crime (until next time).

Christmas Joy

INGREDIENTS

375 grams whole wheat flour
1 teaspoon of baking powder
5 heaped tablespoons of natural peanut butter
2 tablespoons honey
1 egg
Water.

Preheat the oven to 180 degrees. In a large bowl combine all the ingredients then slowly add the water until you have a stiff dough. Flour a work surface and then tip the dough out onto it. Roll out the dough until its 1cm thick and use a cookie cutter of your choice to cut out your treats. If you are going to hang them on the tree remember to use a skewer to make the holes for the ribbon. Place these on a lightly oiled baking tray and bake for about 20 minutes until golden. Leave to cool.

The dogs all get Christmas presents in the form of treats; however Jade and Blue also share a canine advent calendar which is kept in Tabby's bedroom. Both will line up with an expectant air at day break waiting their turn in an oddly patient manner.

They are an interesting mix of both being top dog in their own minds but very conciliatory to each other too ('best be nice to her, poor thing, it must be hard to live up to my greatness..')...advent treats are dished out by respective owners and the day begins.

There is always a sense of impending excitement; once the tree is decorated with all the confiscated ornaments and the dogs banned from the room. The run up to the big day gets more and more frantic. To make life more difficult for myself we always have two Christmas dinners; one Danish on the 24th and an English one on the 25th.

Since every other year I find myself 'sans' everybody on the 25th (children to their Fathers, Richard to his Dad and my Mother out gallivanting with her mafia mob of friends) the whole turkey shebang gets forgotten about and I settle down with the dogs in the living room.

The fire is crackling away nicely and it finds itself closely guarded by various dogs. I surround myself with forbidden foods (wheat, gluten and dairy being the main ones) and have the ultimate luxury of turning the TV on during the day and attempting to do nothing (I am not very good at this). 'We' are quite happy with this arrangement.

The day progresses with various text messages from Tabby and Tilly both getting increasingly high pitched (and yes you can get high pitched in a text) as they open presents and scoff as much chocolate as feasibly possible since Mum isn't around to monitor it.

Having found myself relaxing it always becomes quite an effort to haul my carcass up and outside but I do. The outside dogs are in need of some festive fun too so I just simply open all the gates and let them pour out at speed into our fields. In a manner I am sure is designed to confuse me they all shoot off in differing directions. The naughtier ones go and check if I have left the chickens out (I haven't:), the offspring of Teddy all go and have an impromptu bath by jumping into the water trough and the clever ones come and sit by my side as I perch on a fallen tree stump. From here I dish out pockets of delicious treats as they all now clamor for my attention. It does seem quite a lovely way to spend what could be a lonely day.

Turkey bake

INGREDIENTS

500 grams shredded cooked Turkey
150 grams breadcrumbs made from wheat and gluten free bread
1 egg beaten
2 left over potatoes (roast will do fine as long as it's not too greasy)
150 grams grated carrot
100 grams finely chopped green beans
3 tablespoons water
1 teaspoon Brewer's yeast

Mix all of the ingredients in a large mixing bowl until well combined. Transfer the mixture to a deep oven proof dish (25x30cm) and level out with a spoon.
Bake in a pre-heated oven at 180 degrees C for 25-30 minutes. Take out and leave to cool.

Cut into 5 cm squares and store in an airtight container in the fridge. Serve a couple of squares at a time on top of normal food.

Joyful jerky

INGREDIENTS

50 ml molasses
1 tablespoon dried rosemary
500 grams lamb

The lamb needs to be stripped of all its fat and then sliced into thin strips along the grain.
Combine the molasses and rosemary in a large bowl and then add the lamb making sure all the meat is well covered with the marinade. Leave to marinate for a couple of hours in the fridge.
Now line a baking sheet with foil and place a wire rack on top. Lay the marinated strips on the rack and then cover with any leftover marinade.

Place in a preheated oven at 110 degrees and cook for 4-5 hours. Remove from the oven and leave to cool.. Store for up to a week in an airtight container in the fridge.

HAPPY NEW YEAR!

Printed in Great Britain
by Amazon